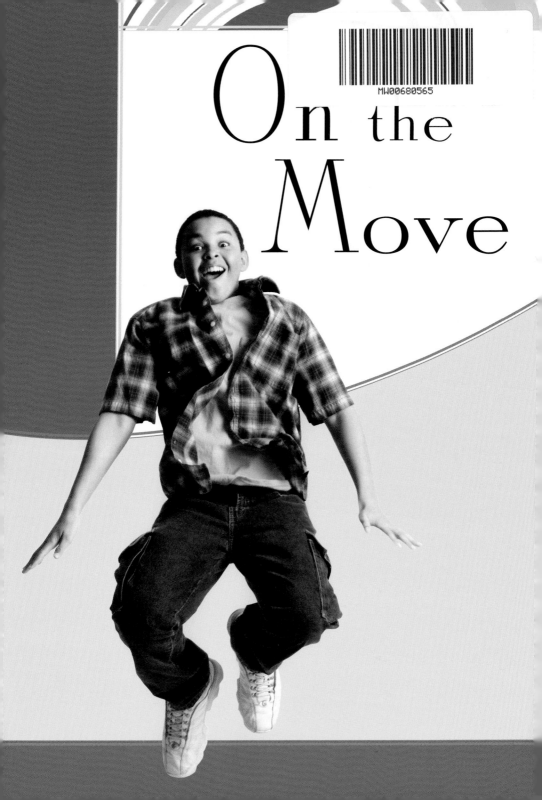

On the Move

Contents

Features

Turn to page 4 to read about a scientist who made an important discovery about energy.

People use electricity constantly in their daily lives, so what happens when the electricity fails? Read page 7 and think about it.

How do people lift very heavy weights? One way is to use a system of pulleys. See for yourself by following the instructions in **Make Your Own Block and Tackle** on page 22.

How does an automobile engine work? Have a look at **The Internal Combustion Engine** on page 25 to find out.

Does gravity exist inside a spacecraft?

Visit **www.rigbyinfoquest.com**
for more about PHYSICS.

Why Things Move

When a ball is thrown into the air, it always comes back down. When the wind blows, it rustles the leaves on the trees. When you use a straw to drink your soda, the liquid travels to your mouth easily. These things might seem very obvious, but they all have one important factor in common—they all use **force.** Without force, the ball would stay in the air, the leaves would remain still, and the straw wouldn't work.

While these forces are different, they all need **energy** to work. Every time something moves, it is a result of energy being used. The science of the properties of matter and energy is called physics.

PROFILE

James Prescott Joule (1818—1889)

James Prescott Joule was an English **physicist** who made the discovery that heat is energy. A unit of energy, the joule, is named after him.

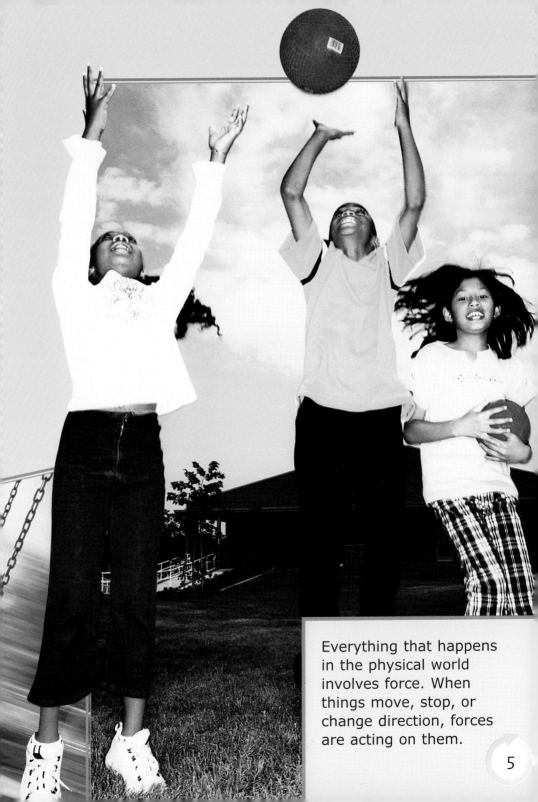

Everything that happens in the physical world involves force. When things move, stop, or change direction, forces are acting on them.

Providing Energy

Forms of Energy

Without energy, absolutely nothing would happen and no life would exist on Earth. Energy is all around us. It cannot be created or destroyed. When people say that energy is being lost, it isn't exactly true. Energy can never be lost and is only changed in some way. This fact is the first law of **thermodynamics**, or the principle of the conservation of energy.

Nuclear Fission

Proton

Uranium atom

Two smaller nuclei

ENERGY

Neutron

Nucleus

Nuclear fission is used to produce electricity in many countries around the world. Nuclear fission is the process of splitting the core, or nucleus, of a uranium **atom.** Splitting an atom releases a huge amount of energy.

Many forms of energy can be generated in a variety of ways. Electrical energy can be produced using the force of the wind or running water, or by burning coal, oil, or other fuels. Electricity is also produced by nuclear power plants.

Life for most people has become almost totally reliant on electricity. Millions of people had to do without it when seven states, including the city of New York, and parts of Canada lost electricity in a blackout on August 17, 2003. Public transportation systems, lights, air-conditioning, and appliances didn't work for nearly 29 hours.

WHAT'S YOUR OPINION?

I think we're too dependent on electricity. When there's a power failure, nothing works! No backup system is foolproof. We have to be more prepared in the future.

The New York City skyline during the August 2003 blackout

Energy Transformation

Before energy can be of much use, it needs to be transformed. This means that one type of energy becomes another type of energy. Energy transformations are taking place around us all the time. When we turn on a light, electrical energy is converted to light energy. When we light a fire, chemical energy is converted to light and heat energy.

Some energy transformations involve many changes. For example, a wind turbine changes wind energy to mechanical energy. This mechanical energy can power a generator which produces electrical energy. That electrical energy can then be transformed into sound energy when we switch on our radios.

Two Examples of Energy Transformations

Source	Device	Change
Chemical energy	burning candle	light and heat energy
Electrical energy	speaker	sound energy

Some energy transformations can damage the environment. When water is used to create hydroelectricity, lakes and rivers can be affected. Burning fossil fuels causes air pollution. Fossil fuels are also in limited supply.

WHAT'S YOUR OPINION?

Nuclear power plants produce dangerous radioactive waste. Fossil fuels aren't the answer to our energy needs either—some scientists say we'll have run out of oil by 2050. I think the energy sources of the future are solar power and wind power. They're clean and renewable.

Solar and wind power aren't the solutions to all our energy needs. They don't provide power in large enough quantities.

Potential and Kinetic Energy

One of the most important types of energy transformation is from potential to **kinetic** energy. Potential energy is the energy that is stored in an object. Kinetic energy is the energy of motion. When a rubber band is stretched, it gains potential energy. When it is released, the potential energy is transformed into kinetic energy.

Kinetic energy is important in creating other forms of energy. Water at the top of a waterfall has potential energy. As it drops down, it is converted to kinetic energy. This kinetic energy can then be used to turn a turbine and produce electrical energy.

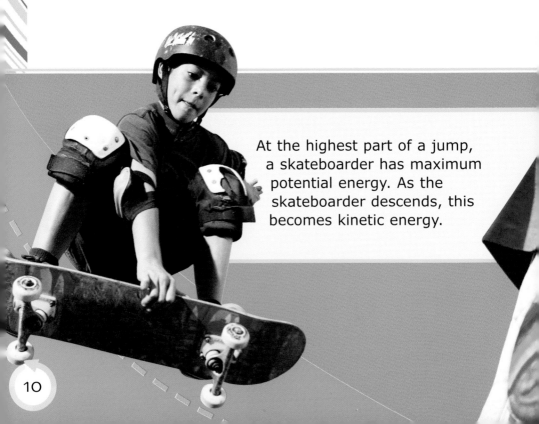

At the highest part of a jump, a skateboarder has maximum potential energy. As the skateboarder descends, this becomes kinetic energy.

When a wound-up yo-yo is held in your hand at a height, it has maximum potential energy. As it falls, the potential energy is gradually converted to kinetic energy. When the yo-yo reaches the bottom of its string, it has no potential energy and maximum kinetic energy.

TRY THIS!

Energy Experiment

You will need:

• a 3x5 inch card

• scissors

• a rubber band

1. Fold the card in half.
2. Cut two slits about an inch deep and an inch apart on each side of the card.
3. Loop the rubber band through the four slits.

4. Flatten out the card. Then let go. What happens?*

*The potential energy in the rubber band is released and becomes the kinetic energy that moves the card.

Consuming Energy

Whether we are running a marathon or quietly reading a book, we are using energy. The more active we are, the more energy we use. Our energy comes from the food we eat. Chemical energy is stored in food. When we eat, our bodies convert this energy into other forms.

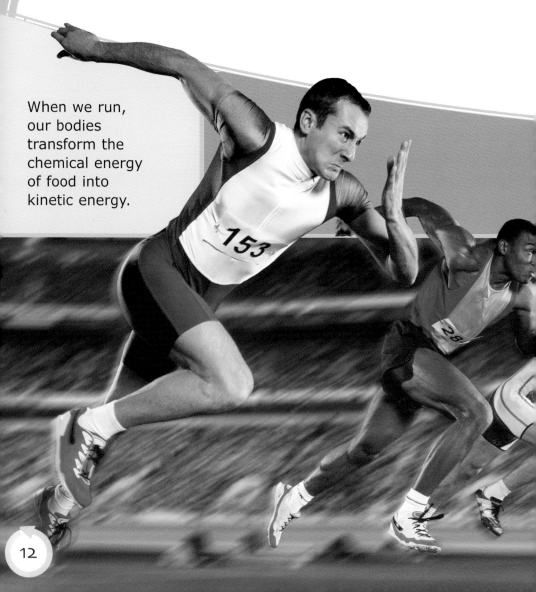

When we run, our bodies transform the chemical energy of food into kinetic energy.

Chemical energy is transformed into electrical energy that our nervous system uses to transmit information from one cell to another, telling muscles to act. Muscles also transform chemical energy into kinetic energy, allowing us to move.

Much of the energy we get from food is turned into heat to keep us warm. A healthy, balanced diet is essential to provide us with the energy we need.

Photosynthesis

Plants get their energy directly from the sun. They transform the sun's **radiant** energy into food in a process called photosynthesis. People get their energy indirectly from the sun by eating plants or by eating animals that have eaten plants.

Radiant energy

Oxygen

Carbon dioxide

Glucose, sucrose, and other carbohydrates are made in the tree's leaves.

Water

Athletes often eat more of certain types of food as they use more energy. Running, swimming, cycling, and other sports require strong muscles, so athletes eat a lot of carbohydrates such as those found in potatoes, bread, rice, and pasta. Carbohydrates are the form of plant energy most easily converted by people into the energy they need.

The more you exercise, the stronger your muscles become. During exercise, the body takes in more oxygen and the heart pumps more blood. You don't need to be a world-class athlete to benefit from exercise. Regular exercise helps every person become fitter, feel better, and enjoy life more.

You might think that more energy is used to ride a bike than to travel in a car, but in fact, traveling a mile by car uses much more energy than traveling a mile by bicycle. The fuel used by cars is not renewable, unlike the fuel used by people—food!

14

Calories and kilojoules are the units used to measure the energy value of food. One calorie equals 4.2 kilojoules.

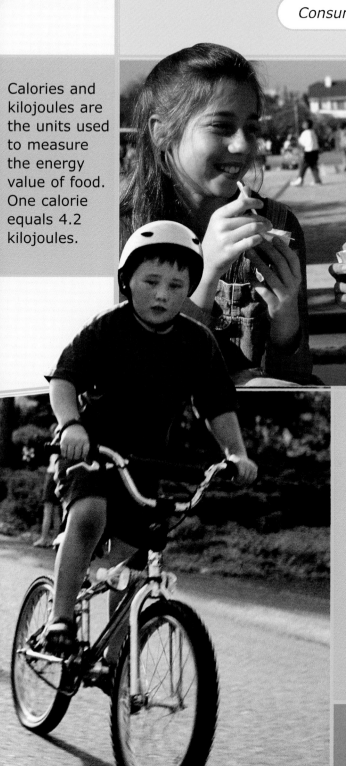

Each 100 kilojoules you consume will give you enough energy to:

- jog for two minutes
- cycle for three minutes
- walk quickly for five minutes
- sleep for half an hour!

15

Forces of Nature

Gravity

All forces use energy either to pull or push an object. Some forces, including the force used when pushing a swing, are easier to understand than others. You can see a person using energy to push the swing.

Other forces are not as easy to see. The swing is either pushed or pulled in one direction, but what force pulls it back in the other direction? This force is called gravity. The force of gravity pulls everything toward the center of Earth. Gravity is what keeps us all from floating into space!

All large bodies such as planets, moons, and stars have gravity, though each planet's gravity is different. Scientists use complex machines such as the gravity wave machine (shown left) to measure gravity on other planets.

The force of hot air rising in one direction overcomes the gravity pulling in the other direction, allowing hot-air balloons to float. Pilots control hot-air balloons by letting more or less hot air into the balloon. Hot air rises and cold air sinks, so the balloon descends when the pilot allows the air to cool.

Gravity

Air pressure

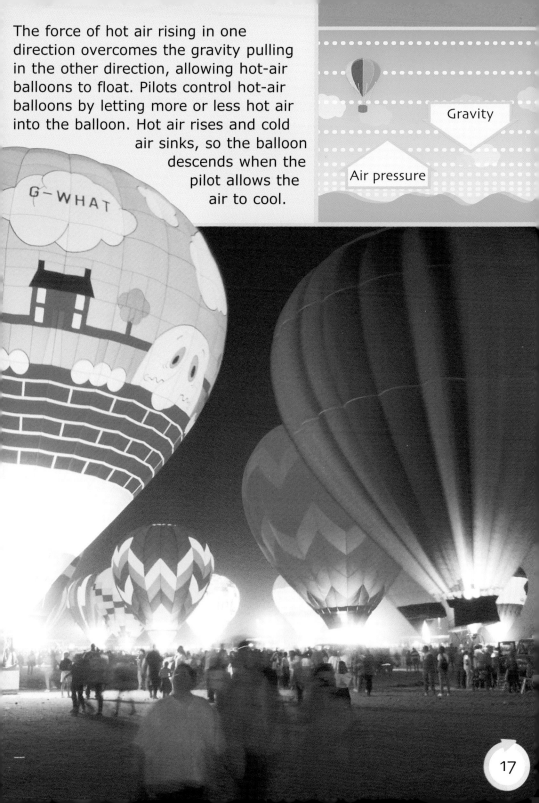

Friction

When the surfaces of objects are rubbed together, a force called friction occurs. Friction is one of the reasons (gravity is another) that we are able to slow down when we are running. Friction is also the reason it takes a lot of energy to speed up. When surfaces are rough, there is more friction. Smooth surfaces such as ice have less friction, so activities such as skating require less energy. Friction can be reduced by using a **lubricant** between surfaces.

Dolphins slip easily through water because their **streamlined** shape minimizes the effect of friction. Friction causes **drag,** which slows objects down. To reduce drag, objects such as yachts, planes, and racing cars are streamlined, too.

Friction and the lack of friction help us in different ways. The oil on a bicycle chain helps reduce friction, so you use less energy to pedal. When you need to brake quickly, your brakes increase friction.

Friction also produces heat. That is why rubbing two sticks together is an ancient way of starting a fire. The sticks become hot and ignite kindling.

In a tug-of-war, friction helps you hold the rope tightly. Your hands are smooth, but the rope is rough.

Combined Forces

Most objects have more than one force acting on them. An airplane, for example, has several forces. Gravity pulls it downward while air beneath the wings lifts it up. **Air resistance** produces a slowing force, or drag, and the engine provides a forward thrust. The combined effect of all these forces is called the **resultant.** The pilot must work out a balance of these forces in order to fly or land the plane.

The force of **buoyancy** keeps boats from sinking, but boats are also affected by the forces of wind and water.

Air resistance acts as a slowing force.

In many situations, forces cancel each other out and the resultant is zero. This means that no overall force is acting and the object is either still or moving at a constant speed. When a pony is pulling a cart at a steady speed, for example, the pulling force of the pony is exactly balanced by the frictional drag between the road and the wheels of the cart. An object whose speed is not changing is said to be in a state of **equilibrium.**

Forces Acting on an Airplane

Engines provide the plane with forward thrust.

Wings provide the plane with lift.

Gravity pulls the plane downward.

Marvelous Machines

Simple Machines

When the word *work* is used in science, it doesn't refer to a job. Work means using a force. Whenever we use our muscles to lift or move something, we are doing work.

We have discovered or invented simple machines to do much of our work for us. These machines use some of the forces found in nature to perform work. Simple machines can be found being used in nearly everything we do. These simple machines include levers, wheels, **pulleys**, ramps, wedges, and screws.

TRY THIS!

Make Your Own Block and Tackle

Pulleys used together are called a block and tackle.

Step 1
Thread a length of string through the holes in two empty thread spools. Tie the ends to a hook.

Step 2
Thread a second length of string through the holes in another two spools, and tie the ends of the string to the handle of a small bucket or other object.

Step 3
Tie a third length of string to the hook. Thread it around the spools, as shown in the illustration. The top spools are the block and the lower spools are the tackle. Pulling the string lifts the bucket.

Levers

Levers help us move weights more easily. They distribute the load to help overcome the force of gravity. A wheelbarrow is a simple machine that uses a lever.

Pulleys

Pulleys change the direction of a force. This helps to overcome gravity. A pulley makes it much easier to pull up a heavy bucket of water from a well.

Wheels

Wheels help us move around more easily. Because only a small part of a wheel is in contact with a surface at any time, it can overcome the slowing force of friction.

Compound Machines

Simple machines are useful by themselves, but they can become very powerful when they are combined. When two or more simple machines are used together, they are called compound, or complex, machines. From cranes to planes and boats to bicycles, these machines make our lives easier.

Under the Hood of an Automobile

Gear shift

Air filter

Battery

Radiator

Engine

Fan

The modern automobile is a good example of a powerful compound machine. Even though the car's design has undergone many changes over the years, the basic principles remain the same. Examples of levers, wheels, pulleys, ramps, wedges, and screws can all be found under the hood of an automobile.

TECHTALK

The Internal Combustion Engine

The principles involved in automobile engines have remained largely unchanged since their invention.

1. The piston descends and sucks in air and fuel.

Spark plug

Exhaust valve

Piston

Intake valve

Piston rod

Crankshaft

2. As the piston rises, the air and fuel are squeezed together.

3. The spark plug causes an explosion in the air/fuel mixture. This pushes the piston down.

4. A valve opens, and the ascending piston forces the exhaust out.

MAGIC MACHINES

TRY THIS!

How do magicians make rabbits pop out of hats? How do they make things disappear? The answers are by using machines! Simple machines, such as levers and pulleys, can be used for surprising effect. This box uses levers to make small objects "disappear"!

How It Works

The trapdoor is opened by a system of levers. When you put the box down, the bottom of the lever pushes up. The top end of the lever is pulled down, taking the front of the trapdoor with it.

Trapdoor

Lever

Now You See It, Now You Don't!

You will need:
- a cardboard box
- paints
- elastic
- glue
- 3 thin wooden rods that are as long as the width of the box
- oaktag or posterboard, the same width as the box but an inch shorter

1. Cut off the top and bottom of a cardboard box. Cut out a triangle in each side to make the front slope down, as in the picture.
2. Add tabs to the oaktag.
3. Pierce a hole at one end of the oaktag and tie a piece of elastic through it. (This will be the false bottom of the box.) Push a rod through each tab underneath the oaktag to support it.
4. Fit the trapdoor 3 inches above the real bottom of the box.
5. Cut a slot in the real bottom of the box.
6. Tape the remaining two rods together at right angles. Tape one end to the underside of the trapdoor. The other end of this rod sticks out through the slot.
7. Push the elastic through the slot and tie it to the rod to keep the trapdoor shut.
8. Paint and decorate the box.

Space Force

What happens to the force of gravity in space? How does work change when the force of gravity is altered or absent? Since the earliest days of spaceflight, scientists have been studying what happens in zero gravity.

Chemicals react differently when there is no gravity. Substances that help in the treatment of diseases such as cancer and diabetes may come one day from experiments in space. Lighter, stronger metals and other new materials can be produced more easily in zero gravity. The possibilities are exciting. Who knows what other technologies will be developed as a result of working in zero gravity?

Effects of Zero Gravity

Floating around in zero gravity sounds like fun, but in fact, lack of gravity has its problems. In zero gravity, the density of bones tends to decrease, and muscles, especially in the legs and back, are weakened. Also, blood moves from the lower half of the body toward the heart and head.

These events can become problems for astronauts when they return to the full gravity of Earth. Scientists are studying ways to lessen these effects.

Tremendous power is needed to overcome Earth's gravity and blast off into space.

USA

United States

Does gravity exist inside a spacecraft?

Visit **www.rigbyinfoquest.com**

for more about PHYSICS.

Glossary

air resistance – friction experienced by an object traveling through air

atom – the smallest particle of a chemical element. Everything in the universe is made up of atoms.

buoyancy – the force that causes an object to float or rise when it is pushed down into a liquid

drag – the slowing force of air or liquid on a moving object

energy – the power which allows work to be done

equilibrium – a state in which opposing forces or influences are balanced

force – a power that causes change in movement

kinetic – to do with movement or caused by movement. Kinetic energy is the energy of a moving object.

lubricant – a substance that reduces the effects of friction

physicist – a scientist who studies physics, the science of matter and energy

pulley – a wheel with a groove around its rim. This simple machine is used to lift very heavy weights.

radiant – transmitted by electromagnetic radiation

resultant – the single force that has the same effect as many forces acting on an object

streamlined – shaped so that air or water flows smoothly over its surface when it is moving. Dolphins are very streamlined.

thermodynamics – the study of heat and work

Index

Research Starters

1 Earth and the other eight planets in our solar system orbit the sun. Find out why this happens.

2 For centuries, people have been searching for a perpetual-motion machine. Find out what *perpetual motion* means. How close are scientists to developing such a device?

3 People use many simple and complex machines to help them do their work. Research to make lists of important simple and complex machines. Which do you consider to be the most important machine ever invented? Give the reasons for your choice.

4 What kinds of fuels are renewable and which of these are being developed now? Why is it important to use renewable fuels whenever possible?